Old COATBRIDGE VILLA

by

Oliver van Helden

The Rochsolloch Ironworks, Coatdyke.

Acknowledgements

Thanks to everyone who helped me out while researching this book, particularly: James Rankin, Badenheath Farm; James Corrigan, Bargeddie; Billy Gardner, Gartcosh; Andrew Montgomery, Mollinsburn; Tommy Gallagher, Carol Ann Kerr, Matthew Hume and the staff of Summerlee Heritage Park; Willie and Rita Smith, Tommy Henvey and Tommy Taylor of Glenboig; Robert Grieves for supplying the pictures that appear on the front cover and page 39, plus information on bus services; and Craig Geddes for reading the manuscript.

Select Bibliography

First, Second and Third Statistical Accounts
The Monklands, An Illustrated Architectural Guide, Allan Peden, 1992
The Raddle (The journal of the Monkland Historical Society)
The Glasgow and Garnkirk Railway, Don Martin, 1981
The Rise and Progress of Coatbridge, Andrew Miller
The Auld Grey Kirk on the Hill, James Lindsay, 1990
The History of Gartcosh, Gartcosh Primary School, 1979
The Growth of the Monklands, George Thomson, 1947
The Scottish Refractory Industry 1830 - 1980, Kenneth Sanderson, 1990
The *Airdrie and Coatbridge Advertiser*

© Stenlake Publishing, 1997
First published in the United Kingdom, 1997
By Stenlake Publishing, Ochiltree Sawmill, The Lade
Ochiltree, Ayrshire KA18 2NX
Telephone / fax: 01290 423114

ISBN 1 84033 012 0

Badenheath Tower, near Mollinsburn, is believed to have been built by the third Earl of Kilmarnock. Stone from the tower was used for the building of Badenheath Farm, *c.*1850, and 100 years later the remains of the tower were demolished and taken to Kilsyth for use as terracing. With walls over six feet thick, this four-storey keep must have made an impressive sight, although by 1887 it was already being described as 'a mere fragment'.

Introduction

In 1793 the author of the Statistical Account for Old Monkland wrote 'A stranger is struck with the view of this parish: it has the appearance of an immense garden'. The rural idyll wasn't to last much longer. Catalysed by the cutting of the Monkland Canal, which provided an effective communication link with Glasgow, coal, iron and fireclay industries began to exploit local mineral wealth on an unprecedented scale.

The fortunes of the Monkland Canal were initially uncertain, but by the early nineteenth century it was demonstrating the profitability of transporting cheap Lanarkshire coal to Glasgow, 'the great commercial emporium of the west'. Following this example (although denying that they intended to compete with the canal), a group of interested landowners and industrialists promoted the Glasgow and Garnkirk Railway. In 1831 this opened up another area of Lanarkshire to the rich city markets. The foundations of a comprehensive transport network had been laid, and by 1840 it was said of Old Monkland Parish that 'The communications in all directions by roads, railways, and the canal, are such as might be expected in a great commercial district'.

Whilst selling coal to Glasgow was profitable, a new and equally large local market developed with the expansion of ironmaking in the Monklands. Around 1805 David Mushet, manager of the Calder Ironworks, is believed to have discovered blackband ironstone. With the subsequent development of the hot blast smelting process in 1828, this rich raw material gave rise to a prodigious iron industry centred around the village of Coatbridge. Coal mines and ironworks enjoyed a mutually beneficial relationship, as Rev. William Thomson observed in 1840: 'if it were not for the ironstone, not one-half of the coals could have been wrought out'. The presence of the canal was also vital, both for supplying water to the various works, and as a means of distributing their products.

Meanwhile, another key Monklands industry owed its inception to the Glasgow and Garnkirk Railway (a railway on which its future success depended). While pits were being sunk around Garnkirk in anticipation of the new railway, deposits of fireclay were discovered. Clay was also located in the Glenboig area to the east of Garnkirk, and by 1888 over 200,000 tons of it were being mined each year. Once again this dovetailed with another Monklands industry; the range of products manufactured included firebricks, a steady supply of which was required to line the furnaces of the local ironworks.

Such rapid industrialisation inevitably led to massive population increases, and in the first of several leaps the number of people living in Old Monkland Parish rose from 1,813 in 1755 to c.4,000 in 1793. The new industries were opportunistic, and works were located wherever the necessary combination of raw materials and transportation could be found, with accommodation for workers usually built alongside. As a result the Monklands' population influx was not directed towards any particular centre. In 1840 Airdrie was named as the nearest market town; the Coatbridge area was described as 'one large village'. The surroundings told a similar story: 'New villages are springing up almost every month, and it is quite impossible to keep pace with the march of prosperity, and the increase of the population'. Coatbridge remained an unconsolidated collection of communities until 1885, and a population of approximately 25,000 people had no proper local government. Overcrowding and lack of pollution controls led to dreadful living and working conditions.

The intensity of the industrial boom in and around Coatbridge couldn't last forever, and some establishments, like the fireclay works in Garnkirk, barely survived the end of the nineteenth century, closing when local supplies of clay were exhausted. A shortage of raw materials created similar problems for the iron industry. Its output peaked c.1870 after which blackband and other poorer locally-available ores were almost worked out.

During the twentieth century, almost all of the industry that was established over the previous 200 years has vanished. Following a period of decay and sky-high unemployment, the fortunes of Coatbridge have improved. The story of the surrounding villages is less straightforward. Annathill virtually disappeared with the demolishing of the old rows, but new housing has since created a middle-class commuter village in its place. With private transport now virtually universal, many of the other villages have also become pit-stops located near the motorway. What was once a localised and intensively industrial community now largely travels to shop and work elsewhere.

Author's note: The label 'Old Coatbridge Villages' has been used with some licence. Coatbridge was the largest community to emerge from the industrial bonanza in and around Old Monkland Parish over the last three centuries. Other villages included in this book were either parties to the boom, or on the periphery of it.

Originally a tiny hamlet, Coatdyke was one of a number of villages that grew up around Coatbridge and were eventually absorbed into the burgh. There was formerly a toll house at the cross, and the *Airdrie and Coatbridge Advertiser* of 4 September 1869 reported an unseemly incident in which the driver of a vehicle refused to pay his dues there. Instead, he 'lifted the toll-gate off its hinges, and proceeded to Low Coats, followed by the tollman and others'. A fight broke out in which the tollkeeper was knocked over, before the defaulter was apprehended and fined ten shillings! All the buildings on the left hand side of Muiryhall Street have been demolished.

Deedes St and Main Street, Coatdyke.

Monklands' industrial explosion was due in no small part to David Mushet's discovery of metal-rich blackband ironstone. Mushet's first experiments used blackband taken from a seam called the Palacecraig, found in the side of a small burn in Coatdyke. The iron industry took off to such an extent that in 1840 Rev. William Thomson wrote that 'Out of the eighty-eight furnaces for the manufacture of iron, which at present exist in Scotland, sixty-five are in this parish [Old Monkland], or in its immediate neighbourhood'. The ironworks lined the canal from Woodside to Coatdyke.

Main Street, Coatdyke.

Coatdyke was put on the map when A.J. Stewart relocated his Glasgow ironfounding business there in the 1860s. This move generated employment and opportunity, but the motivations behind it were less than wholesome. Unlike Airdrie, which attained burgh status in 1821, Coatbridge and its environs had no effective local government and no requirement to control pollution. This is probably what attracted Stewart to Coatdyke and the village suffered doubly, lying as it did downwind of the bulk of the furnaces. Modern Coatdyke is split between the burghs of Airdrie and Coatbridge, and until recently the Boundary Bar, which stood on Main Street across from the junction with Rochsolloch Road, marked the division.

Now demolished, the Stewart Institute stood to the west of the Stewart and Lloyd office building in Coatdyke. The offices, which survive as Monklands District Court, were opened in 1906 and accommodated 140 clerks on the ground floor alone. This gives some idea of the scale of the business, which became the biggest tube manufactory in the world following its move to Coatdyke. At the Imperial Works tubes ranging from one eighth of an inch to six feet in diameter were made. The small fountain at Coatdyke Cross (visible in the picture on page 4) was, ironically, erected by the company to celebrate the occasion of the burgh charter in 1885.

Irvine Crescent, West Entrance, Cliftonville, Coatdyke.

The houses of Cliftonville were built during the inter-war period and laid out in garden-city style. They were known as the intermediate houses after the 'key' workers, such as teachers, that they were designed to attract to the area. Cliftonville is still considered a posher council area.

THIS IS A REAL PHOTO

Residents of Rochsolloch Road, Coatdyke, enjoyed charming views of the ironworks with the same name. These were built in 1858 by Isaiah Clark and James Walker of the Rochsolloch Brickworks. Before the end of the century the iron company underwent repeated changes of ownership and financial crises, although the works survived until 1964. In 1901 it had twenty-six puddling furnaces.

All the old buildings of Kippen Street were demolished after the Second World War. The housing was crumbling and inadequate, and former residents remember outside toilets where a stick was kept to break the ice in winter. The shop on the left was still a greengrocers at the time of demolition in the fifties when it belonged to Joe Beckett.

Rochsolloch Primary, at the top of Kippen Street, is one of the few old buildings to survive. Rochsolloch FC, one of the best amateur football teams in the area, was made up of former pupils.

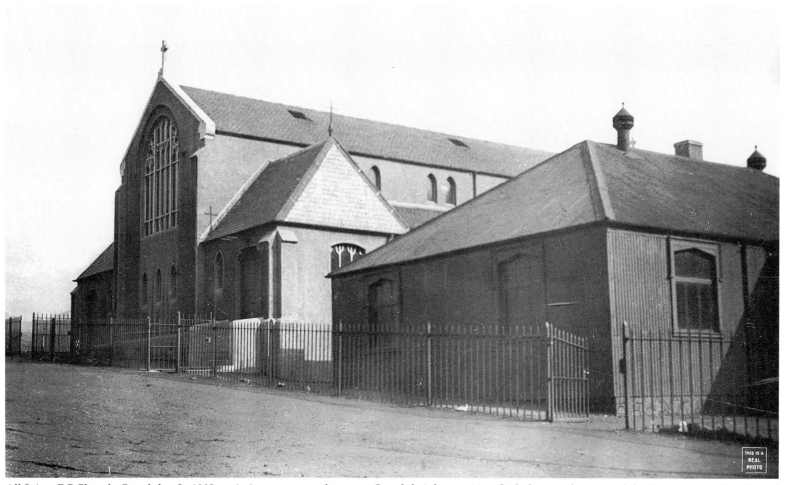

All Saints RC Church, Coatdyke. In 1902 a mission was created to serve Coatdyke's burgeoning Catholic population, and the then priest, Father Daniel Collins, had aspirations to build a fine red sandstone church and presbytery on this site in Saline Street. The presbytery was built first, and initially doubled as church and school, but as a short term measure a temporary brick church (above) was built to accommodate the growing congregation. A more permanent building was never put up. By the seventies the brick church was showing its age, and the old houses in the neighbourhood had been demolished. With the closure of the school and the industrialisation of the surrounding area the original church became more and more isolated, and in 1976 the All Saints congregation moved into the former Church of Scotland Holy Trinity Church in Muiryhall Street.

ALL SAINTS COATDYKE

After a ten year renovation programme, a dedication service was held in Holy Trinity and All Saints in May 1986. The old Chapel House (above) in Saline Street is now burnt out and minus its roof, and the former church is in an advanced state of dilapidation.

OLD SCHOOL, BARGEDDIE

In 1876 the Baird Trust built a church in the small mining village of Bargeddie. The village was chosen in preference to neighbouring Langmuir and Cuilhill because of its central location on a main road, and in 1894 its church was supplemented by a school, which is still in use. A brickworks was established in Bargeddie c.1900. This employed around sixty men and produced four and a half million bricks annually, using clay from an open cast quarry. Special coloured bricks for facing the Stewart and Lloyd's office building in Coatdyke were made by Messrs Dewar and Finlay of Bargeddie. This picture of the 'Old School' is believed to show a building which was later known as Ross's Hall. It may have been a school originally, but at one time it housed a sweetie factory and was later used as a hall for dancing and entertainment.

Bedlay, Glenboig.

The shafts of Bedlay Colliery were sunk by William Baird and Co. in 1905. With its neighbouring coke ovens, Bedlay was established to produce high quality coking coal for the Gartsherrie Iron Works. The colliery employed almost a thousand men in 1969 and produced *c.*250,000 tons of coal annually, but Bedlay closed in December 1981 and the shafts were filled in the following year. Material from the bings was used as bottoming for the M80.

The three rows of houses that comprised most of Annathill were built by William Baird & Co. for workers in Bedlay Colliery and its adjoining coke oven section. Collectively named Annathill Terrace, they were known simply as Front, Middle and Back Row. With the exception of eight larger houses in Back Row, which had three apartments, indoor toilets, and front and back doors, the houses were made up of two rooms - a living room and a bedroom. The scullery, a cupboard with a sink and running water, was in the living room. An upmarket housing development, comprising Annathill Gardens and Bedlay Place, now occupies the site of the rows.

Nowadays Annathill's sole amenity is a post box, but at one time it had a grocers and post office, fish and chip shop, two co-ops, a sweet shop and a cobblers. Leisure facilities included a bowling green (above), tennis court, recreation ground, social club and football pitch. Bedlay's distinguished football team produced four international players, including John 'Tiger' Shaw of Rangers. He captained Scotland, while his brother Davie played for and captained Hibs, and was manager of Aberdeen. The single-storey buildings between the rows contained coal houses on one side and middens on the other. There were small drying greens in between them.

Annathill looking north-west towards Mollinsburn. The Mission Hall can just be made out in the background between the trees. A branch of the Gartsherrie Works Co-op occupied the western end of Middle Row, with the village pub, known as 'The Billy', adjoining it. With the closure of Bedlay, the bulk of Annathill's former mining community was rehoused in Glenboig and Moodiesburn. Since then, the deserted village has gradually been redeveloped with well-to-do private accommodation, and in 1985 disconcerted residents protested about the establishment of a proposed travellers' site. At the time they expressed a desire to be shifted administratively from Monklands to Strathkelvin District. This was unsuccessful, and now that the travellers' site has been built residents have no quarrel with it.

Four bungalows now occupy the site of Annathill Public School. The former Coatbridge Co-op building, bearing the date 1909, stands out of shot to the right of this picture. John C. Sword of Airdrie owned the Midland bus company. He operated a service between Airdrie and Kilsyth which he shared with rival operator John Carmichael. Competition ceased when Midland began to ply a more lucrative route to Paisley and Johnstone from Glasgow.

Dating from 1924, Annathill Mission Hall is still standing - but only just. The minister during the 1960s was a Mr Whitfield, who is remembered as providing musical accompaniment to the services with his concertina. Due to dwindling congregations, the hall closed in 1969. During the early 1980s it was believed to belong to a Mr Dolan, who occupied two caravans near the site. When Annathill Gardens and Bedlay Place were being built in 1996 caravans once again appeared by the hall. A sign, reading PRIVET ROAD, was put up on the approach to it and after a court case disputing right of way the occupants of the caravans were given notice to leave.

The Cross Glenboig

Abundant fireclay deposits around Glenboig and Garnkirk led to the development of a thriving refractory industry during the nineteenth century. Although decorative products were also made from fireclay, its foremost use was in the manufacture of heat-resistant bricks for lining furnaces and hot blast stoves. The top quality clay that was mined in and around Glenboig ensured that the village rapidly developed as a centre for brick-making. By the beginning of this century the world famous Glenboig Union Fireclay Company (comprising the 'Old' Works and the Star Works) was producing an astonishing 250,000 bricks a day. One type of local clay, called Gain Blue, was particularly highly rated. Cracks in bricks could be detected by knocking two of them together, and those made from top-quality Gain Blue were said to 'ring like cheenie'. It is said that the Gain Blue seam was lost during strikes in 1926 when Polish and Lithuanian strike-breakers were unable to follow its course.

Glenboig House.

There was a fireclay works in Glenboig from the 1830s onwards, but it was only later that large-scale exploitation of the clayfields began. James Dunnachie, who came to the village in 1865, was a key player in the expansion of the Glenboig fireclay industry. His house included a picture gallery (on the right, with the raised glass roof), which was converted into a billiard room in 1884. The Chain Mine, one of countless clay mines in the area, ran under the house. When it was noticed that the floors of his house were no longer level, Dunnachie reputedly had brick pillars built in the mine below to stop the subsidence.

Chapel Bank, Glenboig. The row of houses on the left was known as Moss Bank, and the entrance to the Old Works, commonly known as the 'gates', stood beyond it. The works stretched almost a mile northwards from the gates to the grinding mill where clay and sand was crushed. Kilns for firing the clay were originally fuelled by coal gas manufactured by Dunnachie, although during the twenties the Bussey Company produced shale oil and gas (on principles developed by James 'Paraffin' Young), and this new source of gas was used in the kilns. Unfortunately, the flow was erratic and kiln doors were blown off on more than one occasion.

GLENBOIG.

One of the legacies of Glenboig's mining past has been subsidence. Following a minor earthquake during the sixties, undermining led to the Roman Catholic chapel (above, left) becoming so unsafe that it needed to be demolished. A decade later a giant hollow appeared without warning in the playground of St Joseph's school. The building was closed immediately, and the following morning buses took pupils to Muirhead school instead. In the late fifties heavy rain, another catalyst of subsidence, caused a giant gulf to appear in Muir's field (Farm Road). The hole was so big that it required almost 500 tons of waste from the clay works to fill it.

The building in the left foreground was Glenboig's original church, Chryston Parish Church. It became the Masonic Hall during the 1920s. This is a relatively early picture (c.1905), as during the early 1900s the belfry blew off and wasn't replaced. A wooden school building stood behind the hedges in the distance on the left. This was built as a temporary measure when the original school in Farm Road was condemned as unsafe. The temporary school later became Charlie Gillogaly's cinema, manned by chucker-out Micky Reilly who made sure that no-one slipped in without paying! A more substantial brick picture-house was subsequently built by Mr Maxwell, and on Saturday afternoons this ran popular 'Go As You Please' talent competitions.

Morris Place (foreground) has survived, but Garnqueen Square, beyond it, is no longer standing. The rock-hard fireclay was blasted out of the ground using gelignite, and miners brought their explosives home from work with them. One such miner, a lodger in the Wolfes' house in Garnqueen Square, put his damp gelignite in the oven to dry out. Whilst shaving at the window he forgot about it, and when he turned round it was too late to prevent it from exploding. It blew the front of the house away. Safety in the mines was bad enough without such domestic hazards. A 1909 accident called the Star Pit Disaster (which did not occur at the Star) led to the death of several miners. It was rumoured that safety rules had been flouted, and before mines' inspectors arrived on the scene, props which should have been in place previously were put up.

Trains ran through Glenboig round the clock, and Carey's Gates (named after the couple who first operated them), were manned twenty-four hours a day. The steps to the right led to a shed which contained an armchair and fire, where the level crossing attendants sat. During the 1950s round-the-clock duties were performed by three ladies including Nellie McCracken and Annie Tiffany. The building to the left of the gates was a coal ree where coal was stored before being collected and distributed by local coalmen. Victoria Terrace, on the right, has been demolished.

The Springburn to Cumbernauld line is still open, but Glenboig station closed on 11 June 1956. Unlike nearby Garnkirk, fireclay deposits in Glenboig lasted into the twentieth century (and some still remain). The principal works in the village were all in operation until the late fifties, and having undergone modernisation the Star Works survived until the seventies, although latterly it used non-local clay.

Johnstone House was built by the Chapmans, local landowners, in 1902. It is now the club house for Mount Ellen Golf Club.

Glenboig Institute.

The Glenboig Institute opened on Christmas Eve 1904, and the *Airdrie and Coatbridge Advertiser* reported that the village 'was practically "en fete" on the occasion'. The institute contained a billiard room, reading rooms (including a separate ladies recreation and reading room) and a games room. Another victim of subsidence, it was demolished *c.*1960.

Gartcosh Station. Long before there was any village to speak of, a railway line ran through Gartcosh. Like the Monkland Canal, the Glasgow and Garnkirk Railway was conceived to transport cheap coal to the city. The railway opened in 1831, and by 1837 there were three intermediate 'stopping stations' on the line, including one at Gartcosh. Traffic using the stations was described as 'very small' in 1839, and no raised platforms or waiting rooms would have been provided. The presence of the railway, however, prompted William Gray & Co. to establish an ironworks in Gartcosh during the 1860s, when the village proper was born.

A railway line still runs through Gartcosh, although the station closed on 5 November 1962. This picture was taken a few months beforehand. At the opening ceremonies for the Glasgow and Garnkirk Railway the St Rollox locomotive, pulling a train carrying the Airdrie Instrumental Band and 200 guests, left Glasgow for Garnkirk. About halfway along the line the St Rollox met the George Stephenson heading in the other direction with thirty-two waggons in tow. In 1846 this successful line was taken over by the Caledonian Railway, and from 1848 all main line trains heading to Glasgow from London and the Midlands had to pass through Gartcosh.

Towards the end of the nineteenth century the ironworks converted to steel production. Six blocks of company houses (believed to be the terrace in the left foreground) were built in Lochend Road to accommodate people from the original village, plus other skilled workers who were brought into the area. By the late seventies, tenants in many of these houses were being reaccommodated in new properties by Johnstone Loch, and the old buildings were subsequently demolished. The building obscured by trees on the right was a billiard room known as 'The Buggy' and the shop at the far end of the terrace on the right was a cafe and fish and chip shop. Wholesale demolition and the building of the M73 completely wiped out this attractive village centre.

Lochend Rd Looking South, Gartcosh.

Gartcosh Steel Works - as they eventually became known - were one of the village's most enduring employers. During the Second World War the works were largely staffed by women - about 400 in total - and products made there included metal squares which were sent to Sheffield for making helmets. In 1973 Gartcosh was described as 'one of the best equipped plants of its kind in the world', although thirteen years later it had shut down. The Austin belonged to Sam Crawford, the first person in Gartcosh to own a car.

Gartcosh House was built in 1880 by Smith & McLean for the manager of their steel works. The building on right is Chatmans pub, and the lane in the left foreground led to Gartcosh station.

The M73 now cuts a diagonal swathe across Lochend Road. The original iron railway bridge was built in 1830 to carry the Glasgow to Garnkirk Railway across the dirt track leading to Coatbridge, and significantly predated the village.

Lochview Terrace. Iron making wasn't the only industry to locate in Gartcosh following the arrival of the railway, and in 1863 the Gartcosh Fire Clay Works was established. Like many of the neighbouring fireclay companies, Gartcosh produced a variety of ornamental and utilitarian products, ranging from 'tazzas, pedestals [and] fountains' to 'cattle, horse and dog troughs'. The works were in Old Gartcosh Road, on the site of John G. Russell's container base, and operated until the 1950s when supplies of fireclay were exhausted.

Lochend Road prior to the First World War. Now the site of a house, the glasshouses across the loch were Kirby's tomato houses.

One of Alexanders' Leyland buses which operated between Glasgow and Gartcosh. The service was started by Sturrat of Gartcosh in the 1920s and Alexanders' operated it from their depot at Stepps.

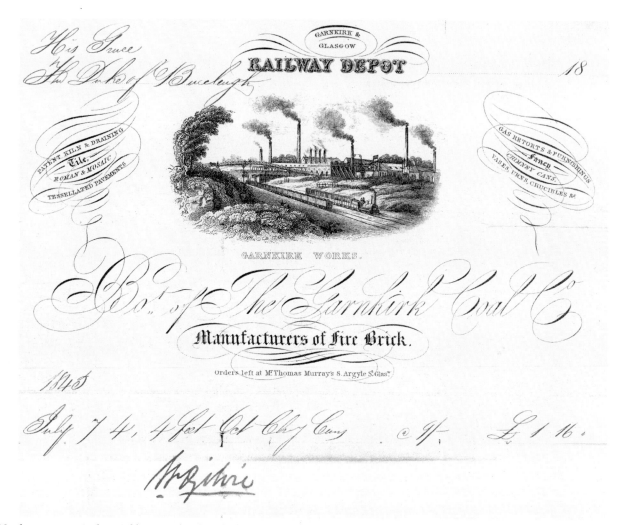

His Grace
The Duke of Buccleugh

GARNKIRK &
GLASGOW

RAILWAY DEPOT

18

PATENT KILN & DRAINING
Tile,
ROMAN & MOSAIC
TESSELLATED PAVEMENTS

GAS RETORTS & FURNISHINGS
Fancy
CHIMNEY CANS
VASES, URNS, CRUCIBLES &c

GARNKIRK WORKS.

Bo.t of The Garnkirk Coal Co

Manufacturers of Fire Brick.

Orders left at Mr Thomas Murray's 8. Argyle St. Glas.w

1845

July 7 4, 4 feet Oct Chy Cans   @ 9/-   £ 1 16.

During the 1830s there was an industrial bonanza in Garnkirk. Coal pits were sunk to coincide with the opening of the Glasgow and Garnkirk Railway in 1831, and in the process rich deposits of fireclay were discovered too. Despite its name, the Garnkirk Coal Company dealt principally in fireclay products, and by 1869 employed over 300 people and consumed around 200 tons each of clay and coal per day. But by 1895 the pits were reaching exhaustion, and although the works continued to operate for a little longer the buildings were advertised for sale in early 1901.

Gartloch Distillery in Chryston was built in 1897-98 by Northern Distillers Ltd. After they went bankrupt in 1900 it was bought by James Calder & Co. who subsequently sold it to Distillers Company Ltd. They closed it down. In December 1920 Scotland held a national referendum on prohibition, an indicator of the hostile climate that the drinks industry found itself in at the time. Following the closure of Garnkirk Fireclay Works at the turn of the century some former Garnkirk workers were employed at the distillery.

The Park, Mollinsburn

660/15

In 1836 the village of Mollinsburn was made up of 'thirty-two families and 172 persons'. The writer of the New Statistical Account wrote that 'it is well suited for wood and water and whinstone rock, and might become a handsome village, were the feu more moderate'. Despite the dramatic boom and bust of nearby Annathill and Bedlay, Mollinsburn has remained a small community. The village's big house formerly belonged to Davie O'Hagan, owner of a sweetie factory in Glasgow.

The old blacksmith's shop in Mollinsburn shut in the 1950s. The smith at the time was Davy Jarvie, and the man in this curious picture is his father.

The shop in the middle distance belonged to Maggie Lang, whilst four generations of the Montgomery family have run the shop at the bottom of the street on the right. Rab Black, owner of the former Mill Garage, was a well-known Mollinsburn personality. A prolific inventor, he made an early 'helicopter' consisting of a box which the passenger stood in, with a propeller on a vertical pole above it. Apparently Rab rose to the height of a telegraph pole in his creation, enough for him to be able to say he had flown. In his shop he had a fully operational scale model of Bedlay pit which he would set in motion for a penny. Rab's talents seem to have been unlimited: he used a windmill behind the garage to generate electricity for small lights in his shop, and also took the credit for inventing the free wheel for bicycles.

East End, Condorrat.

The name Condorrat is believed to derive from the Gaelic *comh dobhair ait* meaning 'joint river place'. Like nearby Cumbernauld, the village was originally a weaving community, although local pits and quarries subsequently employed many people. Condorrat's most famous son is John Baird, one of the ringleaders of the Radical Rising of 1820. Born at Torbrex in 1790, he was living with his brother's family in Condorrat at the time of the rising. Many Scottish weavers found themselves unemployed and impoverished as the Industrial Revolution undermined their livelihoods, and Baird became commandant of the Condorrat Radicals, whose aim was to redress the balance for weavers.

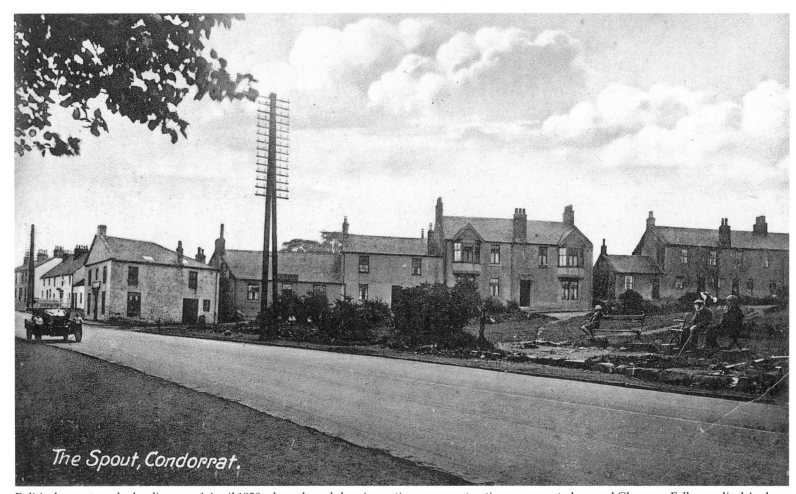

The Spout, Condorrat.

Political unrest reached a climax on 1 April 1820 when placards bearing anti-government notices were posted around Glasgow. Fellow radical Andrew Hardie set off for Condorrat with a group of supporters, where he met up with Baird. From there, the thirty-strong group left for Carron Ironworks, where they expected to be supplied with arms and ammunition. They were intercepted by a group of Hussars *en route*, and eighteen men were captured. After a trial the two ringleaders were hung and beheaded outside Stirling Castle; their supporters were transported to New South Wales. The bay-windowed tenement in MacLean Place marks the site of Baird's house and bears a plaque to his memory. This area of Condorrat was known as 'The Spout' after a spring that used to flow in the park on the right.

Condorrat School stood at the west end of the village on a site now occupied by Woodmill Gardens. The school was built in 1874 and at the turn of the century had 200 pupils and five teachers. Following the Second World War the parish of Cumbernauld found itself at the centre of substantial house-building plans. Apart from the nearby new town, which was defined by the Secretary of State in 1955, 89 old dwellings were condemned and closed in Condorrat by the local authority. These were replaced with extra housing to accommodate the village's growing population.

The building in the background with the iron hoops outside it was Condorrat's blacksmith's shop. This was demolished about thirty years ago and the last smith is believed to have been Mr McAuley. The building in the right foreground is the former co-op. It has survived, along with the two dormered cottages opposite.